SCRIPTURE JOURNAL

ENGLISH STANDARD VERSION

1 CORINTHIANS

CROSSWAY

WHEATON, ILLINOIS — ESV.ORG

ESV® Scripture Journal: 1 Corinthians

The Holy Bible, English Standard Version® (ESV®)
Copyright © 2001 by Crossway,
a publishing ministry of Good News Publishers.
All rights reserved.

ESV® Text Edition: 2016

Printed in China
Published by Crossway
Wheaton, Illinois 60187, U.S.A.
crossway.org

Crossway is a not-for-profit publishing ministry that exists solely for the purpose of publishing the Good News of the Gospel and the Truth of God's Word, the Bible. A portion of the purchase price of every ESV Bible is donated to help support Bible distribution ministry around the world.

The ESV Bible is free online and on mobile devices everywhere worldwide, including a selection of free Bible resources, at esv.org.

RRDS	26	25	24	23	22	21	20	19	18	17
12	11	10	9	8	7	6	5	4	3	2	1

PREFACE

The Bible

The words of the Bible are the very words of God our Creator speaking to us. They are completely truthful;[1] they are pure;[2] they are powerful;[3] and they are wise and righteous.[4] We should read these words with reverence and awe,[5] and with joy and delight.[6] Through these words God gives us eternal life,[7] and daily nourishes our spiritual lives.[8]

The ESV Translation

The English Standard Version® (ESV®) stands in the classic stream of English Bible translations that goes back nearly five centuries. In this stream, accurate faithfulness to the original text is combined with simplicity, beauty, and dignity of expression. Our goal has been to carry forward this legacy for this generation and generations to come.

The ESV is an "essentially literal" translation that seeks as far as possible to reproduce the meaning and structure of the original text and the personal style of each Bible writer. We have sought to be "as literal as possible" while maintaining clear expression and literary excellence. Therefore the ESV is well suited for both personal reading and church ministry, for devotional reflection and serious study, and for Scripture memorization.

---

[1] Ps. 119:160; Prov. 30:5; Titus 1:2; Heb. 6:18 [2] Ps. 12:6 [3] Jer. 23:29; Heb. 4:12; 1 Pet. 1:23
[4] Ps. 19:7–11 [5] Deut. 28:58; Ps. 119:74; Isa. 66:2 [6] Ps. 19:7–11; 119:14, 97, 103; Jer. 15:16
[7] John 6:68; 1 Pet. 1:23 [8] Deut. 32:46; Matt. 4:4

The ESV Publishing Team

The ESV publishing team has included more than a hundred people. The fourteen-member Translation Oversight Committee benefited from the work of fifty biblical experts serving as Translation Review Scholars and from the comments of the more than fifty members of the Advisory Council. This international team from many denominations shares a common commitment to the truth of God's Word and to historic Christian orthodoxy.

To God's Honor and Praise

We know that no Bible translation is perfect; but we also know that God uses imperfect and inadequate things to his honor and praise. So to God the Father, Son, and Holy Spirit—and to his people—we offer what we have done, with our prayers that it may prove useful, with gratitude for much help given, and with ongoing wonder that our God should ever have entrusted to us so momentous a task.

To God alone be the glory!
The Translation Oversight Committee

1 CORINTHIANS

Greeting

1 Paul, called by the will of God to be an apostle of Christ Jesus, and our brother Sosthenes,

² To the church of God that is in Corinth, to those sanctified in Christ Jesus, called to be saints together with all those who in every place call upon the name of our Lord Jesus Christ, both their Lord and ours:

³ Grace to you and peace from God our Father and the Lord Jesus Christ.

Thanksgiving

⁴ I give thanks to my God always for you because of the grace of God that was given you in Christ Jesus, ⁵ that in every way you were enriched in him in all speech and all knowledge— ⁶ even as the testimony about Christ was confirmed among you— ⁷ so that you are not lacking in any gift, as you wait for the revealing of our Lord Jesus Christ, ⁸ who will sustain you to the end, guiltless in the day of our Lord Jesus Christ. ⁹ God is faithful, by whom you were called into the fellowship of his Son, Jesus Christ our Lord.

Divisions in the Church

[10] I appeal to you, brothers, by the name of our Lord Jesus Christ, that all of you agree, and that there be no divisions among you, but that you be united in the same mind and the same judgment. [11] For it has been reported to me by Chloe's people that there is quarreling among you, my brothers. [12] What I mean is that each one of you says, "I follow Paul," or "I follow Apollos," or "I follow Cephas," or "I follow Christ." [13] Is Christ divided? Was Paul crucified for you? Or were you baptized in the name of Paul? [14] I thank God that I baptized none of you except Crispus and Gaius, [15] so that no one may say that you were baptized in my name. [16] (I did baptize also the household of Stephanas. Beyond that, I do not know whether I baptized anyone else.) [17] For Christ did not send me to baptize but to preach the gospel, and not with words of eloquent wisdom, lest the cross of Christ be emptied of its power.

Christ the Wisdom and Power of God

[18] For the word of the cross is folly to those who are perishing, but to us who are being saved it is the power of God. [19] For it is written,

> "I will destroy the wisdom of the wise,
>   and the discernment of the discerning I will
>   thwart."

[20] Where is the one who is wise? Where is the scribe? Where is the debater of this age? Has not God made foolish the wisdom of the world? [21] For since, in the wisdom of God, the

world did not know God through wisdom, it pleased God through the folly of what we preach to save those who believe. [22] For Jews demand signs and Greeks seek wisdom, [23] but we preach Christ crucified, a stumbling block to Jews and folly to Gentiles, [24] but to those who are called, both Jews and Greeks, Christ the power of God and the wisdom of God. [25] For the foolishness of God is wiser than men, and the weakness of God is stronger than men.

[26] For consider your calling, brothers: not many of you were wise according to worldly standards, not many were powerful, not many were of noble birth. [27] But God chose what is foolish in the world to shame the wise; God chose what is weak in the world to shame the strong; [28] God chose what is low and despised in the world, even things that are not, to bring to nothing things that are, [29] so that no human being might boast in the presence of God. [30] And because of him you are in Christ Jesus, who became to us wisdom from God, righteousness and sanctification and redemption, [31] so that, as it is written, "Let the one who boasts, boast in the Lord."

Proclaiming Christ Crucified

2 And I, when I came to you, brothers, did not come proclaiming to you the testimony of God with lofty speech or wisdom. [2] For I decided to know nothing among you except Jesus Christ and him crucified. [3] And I was with you in weakness and in fear and much trembling, [4] and my speech and my message were not in plausible words of wisdom, but in demonstration of the Spirit and of power, [5] so that your faith might not rest in the wisdom of men but in the power of God.

Wisdom from the Spirit

⁶ Yet among the mature we do impart wisdom, although it is not a wisdom of this age or of the rulers of this age, who are doomed to pass away. ⁷ But we impart a secret and hidden wisdom of God, which God decreed before the ages for our glory. ⁸ None of the rulers of this age understood this, for if they had, they would not have crucified the Lord of glory. ⁹ But, as it is written,

> "What no eye has seen, nor ear heard,
>   nor the heart of man imagined,
>   what God has prepared for those who love
>   him"—

¹⁰ these things God has revealed to us through the Spirit. For the Spirit searches everything, even the depths of God. ¹¹ For who knows a person's thoughts except the spirit of that person, which is in him? So also no one comprehends the thoughts of God except the Spirit of God. ¹² Now we have received not the spirit of the world, but the Spirit who is from God, that we might understand the things freely given us by God. ¹³ And we impart this in words not taught by human wisdom but taught by the Spirit, interpreting spiritual truths to those who are spiritual.

¹⁴ The natural person does not accept the things of the Spirit of God, for they are folly to him, and he is not able to understand them because they are spiritually discerned. ¹⁵ The spiritual person judges all things, but is himself to be judged by no one. ¹⁶ "For who has understood the mind of the Lord so as to instruct him?" But we have the mind of Christ.

Divisions in the Church

3 But I, brothers, could not address you as spiritual people, but as people of the flesh, as infants in Christ. ²I fed you with milk, not solid food, for you were not ready for it. And even now you are not yet ready, ³for you are still of the flesh. For while there is jealousy and strife among you, are you not of the flesh and behaving only in a human way? ⁴For when one says, "I follow Paul," and another, "I follow Apollos," are you not being merely human?

⁵What then is Apollos? What is Paul? Servants through whom you believed, as the Lord assigned to each. ⁶I planted, Apollos watered, but God gave the growth. ⁷So neither he who plants nor he who waters is anything, but only God who gives the growth. ⁸He who plants and he who waters are one, and each will receive his wages according to his labor. ⁹For we are God's fellow workers. You are God's field, God's building.

¹⁰According to the grace of God given to me, like a skilled master builder I laid a foundation, and someone else is building upon it. Let each one take care how he builds upon it. ¹¹For no one can lay a foundation other than that which is laid, which is Jesus Christ. ¹²Now if anyone builds on the foundation with gold, silver, precious stones, wood, hay, straw— ¹³each one's work will become manifest, for the Day will disclose it, because it will be revealed by fire, and the fire will test what sort of work each one has done. ¹⁴If the work that anyone has built on the foundation survives, he will receive a reward. ¹⁵If anyone's work is burned up, he will suffer loss, though he himself will be saved, but only as through fire.

¹⁶Do you not know that you are God's temple and that God's Spirit dwells in you? ¹⁷If anyone destroys God's temple,

God will destroy him. For God's temple is holy, and you are that temple.

[18] Let no one deceive himself. If anyone among you thinks that he is wise in this age, let him become a fool that he may become wise. [19] For the wisdom of this world is folly with God. For it is written, "He catches the wise in their craftiness," [20] and again, "The Lord knows the thoughts of the wise, that they are futile." [21] So let no one boast in men. For all things are yours, [22] whether Paul or Apollos or Cephas or the world or life or death or the present or the future—all are yours, [23] and you are Christ's, and Christ is God's.

The Ministry of Apostles

4 This is how one should regard us, as servants of Christ and stewards of the mysteries of God. [2] Moreover, it is required of stewards that they be found faithful. [3] But with me it is a very small thing that I should be judged by you or by any human court. In fact, I do not even judge myself. [4] For I am not aware of anything against myself, but I am not thereby acquitted. It is the Lord who judges me. [5] Therefore do not pronounce judgment before the time, before the Lord comes, who will bring to light the things now hidden in darkness and will disclose the purposes of the heart. Then each one will receive his commendation from God.

[6] I have applied all these things to myself and Apollos for your benefit, brothers, that you may learn by us not to go beyond what is written, that none of you may be puffed up in favor of one against another. [7] For who sees anything different in you? What do you have that you did not receive? If then you received it, why do you boast as if you did not receive it?

⁸ Already you have all you want! Already you have become rich! Without us you have become kings! And would that you did reign, so that we might share the rule with you! ⁹ For I think that God has exhibited us apostles as last of all, like men sentenced to death, because we have become a spectacle to the world, to angels, and to men. ¹⁰ We are fools for Christ's sake, but you are wise in Christ. We are weak, but you are strong. You are held in honor, but we in disrepute. ¹¹ To the present hour we hunger and thirst, we are poorly dressed and buffeted and homeless, ¹² and we labor, working with our own hands. When reviled, we bless; when persecuted, we endure; ¹³ when slandered, we entreat. We have become, and are still, like the scum of the world, the refuse of all things.

¹⁴ I do not write these things to make you ashamed, but to admonish you as my beloved children. ¹⁵ For though you have countless guides in Christ, you do not have many fathers. For I became your father in Christ Jesus through the gospel. ¹⁶ I urge you, then, be imitators of me. ¹⁷ That is why I sent you Timothy, my beloved and faithful child in the Lord, to remind you of my ways in Christ, as I teach them everywhere in every church. ¹⁸ Some are arrogant, as though I were not coming to you. ¹⁹ But I will come to you soon, if the Lord wills, and I will find out not the talk of these arrogant people but their power. ²⁰ For the kingdom of God does not consist in talk but in power. ²¹ What do you wish? Shall I come to you with a rod, or with love in a spirit of gentleness?

Sexual Immorality Defiles the Church

5 It is actually reported that there is sexual immorality among you, and of a kind that is not tolerated even among pagans, for a man has his father's wife. ² And you are arrogant!

Ought you not rather to mourn? Let him who has done this be removed from among you.

³ For though absent in body, I am present in spirit; and as if present, I have already pronounced judgment on the one who did such a thing. ⁴ When you are assembled in the name of the Lord Jesus and my spirit is present, with the power of our Lord Jesus, ⁵ you are to deliver this man to Satan for the destruction of the flesh, so that his spirit may be saved in the day of the Lord.

⁶ Your boasting is not good. Do you not know that a little leaven leavens the whole lump? ⁷ Cleanse out the old leaven that you may be a new lump, as you really are unleavened. For Christ, our Passover lamb, has been sacrificed. ⁸ Let us therefore celebrate the festival, not with the old leaven, the leaven of malice and evil, but with the unleavened bread of sincerity and truth.

⁹ I wrote to you in my letter not to associate with sexually immoral people— ¹⁰ not at all meaning the sexually immoral of this world, or the greedy and swindlers, or idolaters, since then you would need to go out of the world. ¹¹ But now I am writing to you not to associate with anyone who bears the name of brother if he is guilty of sexual immorality or greed, or is an idolater, reviler, drunkard, or swindler—not even to eat with such a one. ¹² For what have I to do with judging outsiders? Is it not those inside the church whom you are to judge? ¹³ God judges those outside. "Purge the evil person from among you."

Lawsuits Against Believers

6 When one of you has a grievance against another, does he dare go to law before the unrighteous instead of the saints? ² Or do you not know that the saints will judge the world? And

if the world is to be judged by you, are you incompetent to try trivial cases? ³ Do you not know that we are to judge angels? How much more, then, matters pertaining to this life! ⁴ So if you have such cases, why do you lay them before those who have no standing in the church? ⁵ I say this to your shame. Can it be that there is no one among you wise enough to settle a dispute between the brothers, ⁶ but brother goes to law against brother, and that before unbelievers? ⁷ To have lawsuits at all with one another is already a defeat for you. Why not rather suffer wrong? Why not rather be defrauded? ⁸ But you your-selves wrong and defraud—even your own brothers!

⁹ Or do you not know that the unrighteous will not inherit the kingdom of God? Do not be deceived: neither the sexually immoral, nor idolaters, nor adulterers, nor men who practice homosexuality, ¹⁰ nor thieves, nor the greedy, nor drunkards, nor revilers, nor swindlers will inherit the kingdom of God. ¹¹ And such were some of you. But you were washed, you were sanctified, you were justified in the name of the Lord Jesus Christ and by the Spirit of our God.

Flee Sexual Immorality

¹² "All things are lawful for me," but not all things are help-ful. "All things are lawful for me," but I will not be dominated by anything. ¹³ "Food is meant for the stomach and the stom-ach for food"—and God will destroy both one and the other. The body is not meant for sexual immorality, but for the Lord, and the Lord for the body. ¹⁴ And God raised the Lord and will also raise us up by his power. ¹⁵ Do you not know that your bod-ies are members of Christ? Shall I then take the members of Christ and make them members of a prostitute? Never! ¹⁶ Or do

you not know that he who is joined to a prostitute becomes one body with her? For, as it is written, "The two will become one flesh." ¹⁷ But he who is joined to the Lord becomes one spirit with him. ¹⁸ Flee from sexual immorality. Every other sin a person commits is outside the body, but the sexually immoral person sins against his own body. ¹⁹ Or do you not know that your body is a temple of the Holy Spirit within you, whom you have from God? You are not your own, ²⁰ for you were bought with a price. So glorify God in your body.

Principles for Marriage

7 Now concerning the matters about which you wrote: "It is good for a man not to have sexual relations with a woman." ² But because of the temptation to sexual immorality, each man should have his own wife and each woman her own husband. ³ The husband should give to his wife her conjugal rights, and likewise the wife to her husband. ⁴ For the wife does not have authority over her own body, but the husband does. Likewise the husband does not have authority over his own body, but the wife does. ⁵ Do not deprive one another, except perhaps by agreement for a limited time, that you may devote yourselves to prayer; but then come together again, so that Satan may not tempt you because of your lack of self-control.

⁶ Now as a concession, not a command, I say this. ⁷ I wish that all were as I myself am. But each has his own gift from God, one of one kind and one of another.

⁸ To the unmarried and the widows I say that it is good for them to remain single, as I am. ⁹ But if they cannot exercise self-control, they should marry. For it is better to marry than to burn with passion.

¹⁰ To the married I give this charge (not I, but the Lord): the wife should not separate from her husband ¹¹ (but if she does, she should remain unmarried or else be reconciled to her husband), and the husband should not divorce his wife.

¹² To the rest I say (I, not the Lord) that if any brother has a wife who is an unbeliever, and she consents to live with him, he should not divorce her. ¹³ If any woman has a husband who is an unbeliever, and he consents to live with her, she should not divorce him. ¹⁴ For the unbelieving husband is made holy because of his wife, and the unbelieving wife is made holy because of her husband. Otherwise your children would be unclean, but as it is, they are holy. ¹⁵ But if the unbelieving partner separates, let it be so. In such cases the brother or sister is not enslaved. God has called you to peace. ¹⁶ For how do you know, wife, whether you will save your husband? Or how do you know, husband, whether you will save your wife?

Live as You Are Called

¹⁷ Only let each person lead the life that the Lord has assigned to him, and to which God has called him. This is my rule in all the churches. ¹⁸ Was anyone at the time of his call already circumcised? Let him not seek to remove the marks of circumcision. Was anyone at the time of his call uncircumcised? Let him not seek circumcision. ¹⁹ For neither circumcision counts for anything nor uncircumcision, but keeping the commandments of God. ²⁰ Each one should remain in the condition in which he was called. ²¹ Were you a bondservant when called? Do not be concerned about it. (But if you can gain your freedom, avail yourself of the opportunity.) ²² For he who was called in the Lord as a bondservant is a freedman of the Lord. Likewise

he who was free when called is a bondservant of Christ. ²³ You were bought with a price; do not become bondservants of men. ²⁴ So, brothers, in whatever condition each was called, there let him remain with God.

The Unmarried and the Widowed

²⁵ Now concerning the betrothed, I have no command from the Lord, but I give my judgment as one who by the Lord's mercy is trustworthy. ²⁶ I think that in view of the present distress it is good for a person to remain as he is. ²⁷ Are you bound to a wife? Do not seek to be free. Are you free from a wife? Do not seek a wife. ²⁸ But if you do marry, you have not sinned, and if a betrothed woman marries, she has not sinned. Yet those who marry will have worldly troubles, and I would spare you that. ²⁹ This is what I mean, brothers: the appointed time has grown very short. From now on, let those who have wives live as though they had none, ³⁰ and those who mourn as though they were not mourning, and those who rejoice as though they were not rejoicing, and those who buy as though they had no goods, ³¹ and those who deal with the world as though they had no dealings with it. For the present form of this world is passing away.

³² I want you to be free from anxieties. The unmarried man is anxious about the things of the Lord, how to please the Lord. ³³ But the married man is anxious about worldly things, how to please his wife, ³⁴ and his interests are divided. And the unmarried or betrothed woman is anxious about the things of the Lord, how to be holy in body and spirit. But the married woman is anxious about worldly things, how to please her husband. ³⁵ I say this for your own benefit, not to lay any restraint

upon you, but to promote good order and to secure your undivided devotion to the Lord.

[36] If anyone thinks that he is not behaving properly toward his betrothed, if his passions are strong, and it has to be, let him do as he wishes: let them marry—it is no sin. [37] But whoever is firmly established in his heart, being under no necessity but having his desire under control, and has determined this in his heart, to keep her as his betrothed, he will do well. [38] So then he who marries his betrothed does well, and he who refrains from marriage will do even better.

[39] A wife is bound to her husband as long as he lives. But if her husband dies, she is free to be married to whom she wishes, only in the Lord. [40] Yet in my judgment she is happier if she remains as she is. And I think that I too have the Spirit of God.

Food Offered to Idols

8 Now concerning food offered to idols: we know that "all of us possess knowledge." This "knowledge" puffs up, but love builds up. [2] If anyone imagines that he knows something, he does not yet know as he ought to know. [3] But if anyone loves God, he is known by God.

[4] Therefore, as to the eating of food offered to idols, we know that "an idol has no real existence," and that "there is no God but one." [5] For although there may be so-called gods in heaven or on earth—as indeed there are many "gods" and many "lords"— [6] yet for us there is one God, the Father, from whom are all things and for whom we exist, and one Lord, Jesus Christ, through whom are all things and through whom we exist.

[7] However, not all possess this knowledge. But some, through former association with idols, eat food as really offered

to an idol, and their conscience, being weak, is defiled. ⁸ Food will not commend us to God. We are no worse off if we do not eat, and no better off if we do. ⁹ But take care that this right of yours does not somehow become a stumbling block to the weak. ¹⁰ For if anyone sees you who have knowledge eating in an idol's temple, will he not be encouraged, if his conscience is weak, to eat food offered to idols? ¹¹ And so by your knowledge this weak person is destroyed, the brother for whom Christ died. ¹² Thus, sinning against your brothers and wounding their conscience when it is weak, you sin against Christ. ¹³ Therefore, if food makes my brother stumble, I will never eat meat, lest I make my brother stumble.

Paul Surrenders His Rights

9 Am I not free? Am I not an apostle? Have I not seen Jesus our Lord? Are not you my workmanship in the Lord? ² If to others I am not an apostle, at least I am to you, for you are the seal of my apostleship in the Lord.

³ This is my defense to those who would examine me. ⁴ Do we not have the right to eat and drink? ⁵ Do we not have the right to take along a believing wife, as do the other apostles and the brothers of the Lord and Cephas? ⁶ Or is it only Barnabas and I who have no right to refrain from working for a living? ⁷ Who serves as a soldier at his own expense? Who plants a vineyard without eating any of its fruit? Or who tends a flock without getting some of the milk?

⁸ Do I say these things on human authority? Does not the Law say the same? ⁹ For it is written in the Law of Moses, "You shall not muzzle an ox when it treads out the grain." Is it for oxen that God is concerned? ¹⁰ Does he not certainly speak for

our sake? It was written for our sake, because the plowman should plow in hope and the thresher thresh in hope of sharing in the crop. [11] If we have sown spiritual things among you, is it too much if we reap material things from you? [12] If others share this rightful claim on you, do not we even more?

Nevertheless, we have not made use of this right, but we endure anything rather than put an obstacle in the way of the gospel of Christ. [13] Do you not know that those who are employed in the temple service get their food from the temple, and those who serve at the altar share in the sacrificial offerings? [14] In the same way, the Lord commanded that those who proclaim the gospel should get their living by the gospel.

[15] But I have made no use of any of these rights, nor am I writing these things to secure any such provision. For I would rather die than have anyone deprive me of my ground for boasting. [16] For if I preach the gospel, that gives me no ground for boasting. For necessity is laid upon me. Woe to me if I do not preach the gospel! [17] For if I do this of my own will, I have a reward, but if not of my own will, I am still entrusted with a stewardship. [18] What then is my reward? That in my preaching I may present the gospel free of charge, so as not to make full use of my right in the gospel.

[19] For though I am free from all, I have made myself a servant to all, that I might win more of them. [20] To the Jews I became as a Jew, in order to win Jews. To those under the law I became as one under the law (though not being myself under the law) that I might win those under the law. [21] To those outside the law I became as one outside the law (not being outside the law of God but under the law of Christ) that I might win those outside the law. [22] To the weak I became weak, that I might win the

weak. I have become all things to all people, that by all means I might save some. ²³ I do it all for the sake of the gospel, that I may share with them in its blessings.

²⁴ Do you not know that in a race all the runners run, but only one receives the prize? So run that you may obtain it. ²⁵ Every athlete exercises self-control in all things. They do it to receive a perishable wreath, but we an imperishable. ²⁶ So I do not run aimlessly; I do not box as one beating the air. ²⁷ But I discipline my body and keep it under control, lest after preaching to others I myself should be disqualified.

Warning Against Idolatry

10 For I do not want you to be unaware, brothers, that our fathers were all under the cloud, and all passed through the sea, ² and all were baptized into Moses in the cloud and in the sea, ³ and all ate the same spiritual food, ⁴ and all drank the same spiritual drink. For they drank from the spiritual Rock that followed them, and the Rock was Christ. ⁵ Nevertheless, with most of them God was not pleased, for they were overthrown in the wilderness.

⁶ Now these things took place as examples for us, that we might not desire evil as they did. ⁷ Do not be idolaters as some of them were; as it is written, "The people sat down to eat and drink and rose up to play." ⁸ We must not indulge in sexual immorality as some of them did, and twenty-three thousand fell in a single day. ⁹ We must not put Christ to the test, as some of them did and were destroyed by serpents, ¹⁰ nor grumble, as some of them did and were destroyed by the Destroyer. ¹¹ Now these things happened to them as an example, but they were written down for our instruction, on whom the end of the ages

has come. [12] Therefore let anyone who thinks that he stands take heed lest he fall. [13] No temptation has overtaken you that is not common to man. God is faithful, and he will not let you be tempted beyond your ability, but with the temptation he will also provide the way of escape, that you may be able to endure it.

[14] Therefore, my beloved, flee from idolatry. [15] I speak as to sensible people; judge for yourselves what I say. [16] The cup of blessing that we bless, is it not a participation in the blood of Christ? The bread that we break, is it not a participation in the body of Christ? [17] Because there is one bread, we who are many are one body, for we all partake of the one bread. [18] Consider the people of Israel: are not those who eat the sacrifices participants in the altar? [19] What do I imply then? That food offered to idols is anything, or that an idol is anything? [20] No, I imply that what pagans sacrifice they offer to demons and not to God. I do not want you to be participants with demons. [21] You cannot drink the cup of the Lord and the cup of demons. You cannot partake of the table of the Lord and the table of demons. [22] Shall we provoke the Lord to jealousy? Are we stronger than he?

Do All to the Glory of God

[23] "All things are lawful," but not all things are helpful. "All things are lawful," but not all things build up. [24] Let no one seek his own good, but the good of his neighbor. [25] Eat whatever is sold in the meat market without raising any question on the ground of conscience. [26] For "the earth is the Lord's, and the fullness thereof." [27] If one of the unbelievers invites you to dinner and you are disposed to go, eat whatever is set before you without raising any question on the ground of conscience. [28] But if someone says to you, "This has been offered in sacrifice," then

do not eat it, for the sake of the one who informed you, and for the sake of conscience— ²⁹ I do not mean your conscience, but his. For why should my liberty be determined by someone else's conscience? ³⁰ If I partake with thankfulness, why am I denounced because of that for which I give thanks?

³¹ So, whether you eat or drink, or whatever you do, do all to the glory of God. ³² Give no offense to Jews or to Greeks or to the church of God, ³³ just as I try to please everyone in everything I do, not seeking my own advantage, but that of many, that they may be saved.

11 Be imitators of me, as I am of Christ.

Head Coverings

² Now I commend you because you remember me in everything and maintain the traditions even as I delivered them to you. ³ But I want you to understand that the head of every man is Christ, the head of a wife is her husband, and the head of Christ is God. ⁴ Every man who prays or prophesies with his head covered dishonors his head, ⁵ but every wife who prays or prophesies with her head uncovered dishonors her head, since it is the same as if her head were shaven. ⁶ For if a wife will not cover her head, then she should cut her hair short. But since it is disgraceful for a wife to cut off her hair or shave her head, let her cover her head. ⁷ For a man ought not to cover his head, since he is the image and glory of God, but woman is the glory of man. ⁸ For man was not made from woman, but woman from man. ⁹ Neither was man created for woman, but woman for man. ¹⁰ That is why a wife ought to have a symbol of authority on her head, because of the angels. ¹¹ Nevertheless, in the

Lord woman is not independent of man nor man of woman; [12] for as woman was made from man, so man is now born of woman. And all things are from God. [13] Judge for yourselves: is it proper for a wife to pray to God with her head uncovered? [14] Does not nature itself teach you that if a man wears long hair it is a disgrace for him, [15] but if a woman has long hair, it is her glory? For her hair is given to her for a covering. [16] If anyone is inclined to be contentious, we have no such practice, nor do the churches of God.

The Lord's Supper

[17] But in the following instructions I do not commend you, because when you come together it is not for the better but for the worse. [18] For, in the first place, when you come together as a church, I hear that there are divisions among you. And I believe it in part, [19] for there must be factions among you in order that those who are genuine among you may be recognized. [20] When you come together, it is not the Lord's supper that you eat. [21] For in eating, each one goes ahead with his own meal. One goes hungry, another gets drunk. [22] What! Do you not have houses to eat and drink in? Or do you despise the church of God and humiliate those who have nothing? What shall I say to you? Shall I commend you in this? No, I will not.

[23] For I received from the Lord what I also delivered to you, that the Lord Jesus on the night when he was betrayed took bread, [24] and when he had given thanks, he broke it, and said, "This is my body, which is for you. Do this in remembrance of me." [25] In the same way also he took the cup, after supper, saying, "This cup is the new covenant in my blood. Do this, as often as you drink it, in remembrance of me." [26] For as often as

you eat this bread and drink the cup, you proclaim the Lord's death until he comes.

²⁷ Whoever, therefore, eats the bread or drinks the cup of the Lord in an unworthy manner will be guilty concerning the body and blood of the Lord. ²⁸ Let a person examine himself, then, and so eat of the bread and drink of the cup. ²⁹ For anyone who eats and drinks without discerning the body eats and drinks judgment on himself. ³⁰ That is why many of you are weak and ill, and some have died. ³¹ But if we judged ourselves truly, we would not be judged. ³² But when we are judged by the Lord, we are disciplined so that we may not be condemned along with the world.

³³ So then, my brothers, when you come together to eat, wait for one another— ³⁴ if anyone is hungry, let him eat at home— so that when you come together it will not be for judgment. About the other things I will give directions when I come.

Spiritual Gifts

12 Now concerning spiritual gifts, brothers, I do not want you to be uninformed. ² You know that when you were pagans you were led astray to mute idols, however you were led. ³ Therefore I want you to understand that no one speaking in the Spirit of God ever says "Jesus is accursed!" and no one can say "Jesus is Lord" except in the Holy Spirit.

⁴ Now there are varieties of gifts, but the same Spirit; ⁵ and there are varieties of service, but the same Lord; ⁶ and there are varieties of activities, but it is the same God who empowers them all in everyone. ⁷ To each is given the manifestation of the Spirit for the common good. ⁸ For to one is given through the Spirit the utterance of wisdom, and to another the utterance of

knowledge according to the same Spirit, [9] to another faith by the same Spirit, to another gifts of healing by the one Spirit, [10] to another the working of miracles, to another prophecy, to another the ability to distinguish between spirits, to another various kinds of tongues, to another the interpretation of tongues. [11] All these are empowered by one and the same Spirit, who apportions to each one individually as he wills.

One Body with Many Members

[12] For just as the body is one and has many members, and all the members of the body, though many, are one body, so it is with Christ. [13] For in one Spirit we were all baptized into one body—Jews or Greeks, slaves or free—and all were made to drink of one Spirit.

[14] For the body does not consist of one member but of many. [15] If the foot should say, "Because I am not a hand, I do not belong to the body," that would not make it any less a part of the body. [16] And if the ear should say, "Because I am not an eye, I do not belong to the body," that would not make it any less a part of the body. [17] If the whole body were an eye, where would be the sense of hearing? If the whole body were an ear, where would be the sense of smell? [18] But as it is, God arranged the members in the body, each one of them, as he chose. [19] If all were a single member, where would the body be? [20] As it is, there are many parts, yet one body.

[21] The eye cannot say to the hand, "I have no need of you," nor again the head to the feet, "I have no need of you." [22] On the contrary, the parts of the body that seem to be weaker are indispensable, [23] and on those parts of the body that we think less honorable we bestow the greater honor, and our unpresentable

parts are treated with greater modesty, [24] which our more presentable parts do not require. But God has so composed the body, giving greater honor to the part that lacked it, [25] that there may be no division in the body, but that the members may have the same care for one another. [26] If one member suffers, all suffer together; if one member is honored, all rejoice together.

[27] Now you are the body of Christ and individually members of it. [28] And God has appointed in the church first apostles, second prophets, third teachers, then miracles, then gifts of healing, helping, administrating, and various kinds of tongues. [29] Are all apostles? Are all prophets? Are all teachers? Do all work miracles? [30] Do all possess gifts of healing? Do all speak with tongues? Do all interpret? [31] But earnestly desire the higher gifts.

And I will show you a still more excellent way.

The Way of Love

13 If I speak in the tongues of men and of angels, but have not love, I am a noisy gong or a clanging cymbal. [2] And if I have prophetic powers, and understand all mysteries and all knowledge, and if I have all faith, so as to remove mountains, but have not love, I am nothing. [3] If I give away all I have, and if I deliver up my body to be burned, but have not love, I gain nothing.

[4] Love is patient and kind; love does not envy or boast; it is not arrogant [5] or rude. It does not insist on its own way; it is not irritable or resentful; [6] it does not rejoice at wrongdoing, but rejoices with the truth. [7] Love bears all things, believes all things, hopes all things, endures all things.

⁸ Love never ends. As for prophecies, they will pass away; as for tongues, they will cease; as for knowledge, it will pass away. ⁹ For we know in part and we prophesy in part, ¹⁰ but when the perfect comes, the partial will pass away. ¹¹ When I was a child, I spoke like a child, I thought like a child, I reasoned like a child. When I became a man, I gave up childish ways. ¹² For now we see in a mirror dimly, but then face to face. Now I know in part; then I shall know fully, even as I have been fully known.

¹³ So now faith, hope, and love abide, these three; but the greatest of these is love.

Prophecy and Tongues

14 Pursue love, and earnestly desire the spiritual gifts, especially that you may prophesy. ² For one who speaks in a tongue speaks not to men but to God; for no one understands him, but he utters mysteries in the Spirit. ³ On the other hand, the one who prophesies speaks to people for their upbuilding and encouragement and consolation. ⁴ The one who speaks in a tongue builds up himself, but the one who prophesies builds up the church. ⁵ Now I want you all to speak in tongues, but even more to prophesy. The one who prophesies is greater than the one who speaks in tongues, unless someone interprets, so that the church may be built up.

⁶ Now, brothers, if I come to you speaking in tongues, how will I benefit you unless I bring you some revelation or knowledge or prophecy or teaching? ⁷ If even lifeless instruments, such as the flute or the harp, do not give distinct notes, how will anyone know what is played? ⁸ And if the bugle gives an indistinct sound, who will get ready for battle? ⁹ So with yourselves, if with your tongue you utter speech that is not intelligible,

how will anyone know what is said? For you will be speaking into the air. [10] There are doubtless many different languages in the world, and none is without meaning, [11] but if I do not know the meaning of the language, I will be a foreigner to the speaker and the speaker a foreigner to me. [12] So with yourselves, since you are eager for manifestations of the Spirit, strive to excel in building up the church.

[13] Therefore, one who speaks in a tongue should pray that he may interpret. [14] For if I pray in a tongue, my spirit prays but my mind is unfruitful. [15] What am I to do? I will pray with my spirit, but I will pray with my mind also; I will sing praise with my spirit, but I will sing with my mind also. [16] Otherwise, if you give thanks with your spirit, how can anyone in the position of an outsider say "Amen" to your thanksgiving when he does not know what you are saying? [17] For you may be giving thanks well enough, but the other person is not being built up. [18] I thank God that I speak in tongues more than all of you. [19] Nevertheless, in church I would rather speak five words with my mind in order to instruct others, than ten thousand words in a tongue.

[20] Brothers, do not be children in your thinking. Be infants in evil, but in your thinking be mature. [21] In the Law it is written, "By people of strange tongues and by the lips of foreigners will I speak to this people, and even then they will not listen to me, says the Lord." [22] Thus tongues are a sign not for believers but for unbelievers, while prophecy is a sign not for unbelievers but for believers. [23] If, therefore, the whole church comes together and all speak in tongues, and outsiders or unbelievers enter, will they not say that you are out of your minds? [24] But if all prophesy, and an unbeliever or outsider enters, he

is convicted by all, he is called to account by all, [25] the secrets of his heart are disclosed, and so, falling on his face, he will worship God and declare that God is really among you.

Orderly Worship

[26] What then, brothers? When you come together, each one has a hymn, a lesson, a revelation, a tongue, or an interpretation. Let all things be done for building up. [27] If any speak in a tongue, let there be only two or at most three, and each in turn, and let someone interpret. [28] But if there is no one to interpret, let each of them keep silent in church and speak to himself and to God. [29] Let two or three prophets speak, and let the others weigh what is said. [30] If a revelation is made to another sitting there, let the first be silent. [31] For you can all prophesy one by one, so that all may learn and all be encouraged, [32] and the spirits of prophets are subject to prophets. [33] For God is not a God of confusion but of peace.

As in all the churches of the saints, [34] the women should keep silent in the churches. For they are not permitted to speak, but should be in submission, as the Law also says. [35] If there is anything they desire to learn, let them ask their husbands at home. For it is shameful for a woman to speak in church.

[36] Or was it from you that the word of God came? Or are you the only ones it has reached? [37] If anyone thinks that he is a prophet, or spiritual, he should acknowledge that the things I am writing to you are a command of the Lord. [38] If anyone does not recognize this, he is not recognized. [39] So, my brothers, earnestly desire to prophesy, and do not forbid speaking in tongues. [40] But all things should be done decently and in order.

The Resurrection of Christ

15 Now I would remind you, brothers, of the gospel I preached to you, which you received, in which you stand, ² and by which you are being saved, if you hold fast to the word I preached to you—unless you believed in vain.

³ For I delivered to you as of first importance what I also received: that Christ died for our sins in accordance with the Scriptures, ⁴ that he was buried, that he was raised on the third day in accordance with the Scriptures, ⁵ and that he appeared to Cephas, then to the twelve. ⁶ Then he appeared to more than five hundred brothers at one time, most of whom are still alive, though some have fallen asleep. ⁷ Then he appeared to James, then to all the apostles. ⁸ Last of all, as to one untimely born, he appeared also to me. ⁹ For I am the least of the apostles, unworthy to be called an apostle, because I persecuted the church of God. ¹⁰ But by the grace of God I am what I am, and his grace toward me was not in vain. On the contrary, I worked harder than any of them, though it was not I, but the grace of God that is with me. ¹¹ Whether then it was I or they, so we preach and so you believed.

The Resurrection of the Dead

¹² Now if Christ is proclaimed as raised from the dead, how can some of you say that there is no resurrection of the dead? ¹³ But if there is no resurrection of the dead, then not even Christ has been raised. ¹⁴ And if Christ has not been raised, then our preaching is in vain and your faith is in vain. ¹⁵ We are even found to be misrepresenting God, because we testified about God that he raised Christ, whom he did not raise if it is true that the dead are not raised. ¹⁶ For if the dead are not raised, not even Christ

has been raised. [17] And if Christ has not been raised, your faith is futile and you are still in your sins. [18] Then those also who have fallen asleep in Christ have perished. [19] If in Christ we have hope in this life only, we are of all people most to be pitied.

[20] But in fact Christ has been raised from the dead, the first-fruits of those who have fallen asleep. [21] For as by a man came death, by a man has come also the resurrection of the dead. [22] For as in Adam all die, so also in Christ shall all be made alive. [23] But each in his own order: Christ the firstfruits, then at his coming those who belong to Christ. [24] Then comes the end, when he delivers the kingdom to God the Father after destroying every rule and every authority and power. [25] For he must reign until he has put all his enemies under his feet. [26] The last enemy to be destroyed is death. [27] For "God has put all things in subjection under his feet." But when it says, "all things are put in subjection," it is plain that he is excepted who put all things in subjection under him. [28] When all things are subjected to him, then the Son himself will also be subjected to him who put all things in subjection under him, that God may be all in all.

[29] Otherwise, what do people mean by being baptized on behalf of the dead? If the dead are not raised at all, why are people baptized on their behalf? [30] Why are we in danger every hour? [31] I protest, brothers, by my pride in you, which I have in Christ Jesus our Lord, I die every day! [32] What do I gain if, humanly speaking, I fought with beasts at Ephesus? If the dead are not raised, "Let us eat and drink, for tomorrow we die." [33] Do not be deceived: "Bad company ruins good morals." [34] Wake up from your drunken stupor, as is right, and do not go on sinning. For some have no knowledge of God. I say this to your shame.

The Resurrection Body

³⁵ But someone will ask, "How are the dead raised? With what kind of body do they come?" ³⁶ You foolish person! What you sow does not come to life unless it dies. ³⁷ And what you sow is not the body that is to be, but a bare kernel, perhaps of wheat or of some other grain. ³⁸ But God gives it a body as he has chosen, and to each kind of seed its own body. ³⁹ For not all flesh is the same, but there is one kind for humans, another for animals, another for birds, and another for fish. ⁴⁰ There are heavenly bodies and earthly bodies, but the glory of the heavenly is of one kind, and the glory of the earthly is of another. ⁴¹ There is one glory of the sun, and another glory of the moon, and another glory of the stars; for star differs from star in glory.

⁴² So is it with the resurrection of the dead. What is sown is perishable; what is raised is imperishable. ⁴³ It is sown in dishonor; it is raised in glory. It is sown in weakness; it is raised in power. ⁴⁴ It is sown a natural body; it is raised a spiritual body. If there is a natural body, there is also a spiritual body. ⁴⁵ Thus it is written, "The first man Adam became a living being"; the last Adam became a life-giving spirit. ⁴⁶ But it is not the spiritual that is first but the natural, and then the spiritual. ⁴⁷ The first man was from the earth, a man of dust; the second man is from heaven. ⁴⁸ As was the man of dust, so also are those who are of the dust, and as is the man of heaven, so also are those who are of heaven. ⁴⁹ Just as we have borne the image of the man of dust, we shall also bear the image of the man of heaven.

Mystery and Victory

⁵⁰ I tell you this, brothers: flesh and blood cannot inherit the kingdom of God, nor does the perishable inherit the

imperishable. **51** Behold! I tell you a mystery. We shall not all sleep, but we shall all be changed, **52** in a moment, in the twinkling of an eye, at the last trumpet. For the trumpet will sound, and the dead will be raised imperishable, and we shall be changed. **53** For this perishable body must put on the imperishable, and this mortal body must put on immortality. **54** When the perishable puts on the imperishable, and the mortal puts on immortality, then shall come to pass the saying that is written:

> "Death is swallowed up in victory."
> **55**   "O death, where is your victory?
>   O death, where is your sting?"

56 The sting of death is sin, and the power of sin is the law. **57** But thanks be to God, who gives us the victory through our Lord Jesus Christ.

58 Therefore, my beloved brothers, be steadfast, immovable, always abounding in the work of the Lord, knowing that in the Lord your labor is not in vain.

The Collection for the Saints

16 Now concerning the collection for the saints: as I directed the churches of Galatia, so you also are to do. **2** On the first day of every week, each of you is to put something aside and store it up, as he may prosper, so that there will be no collecting when I come. **3** And when I arrive, I will send those whom you accredit by letter to carry your gift to Jerusalem. **4** If it seems advisable that I should go also, they will accompany me.

Plans for Travel

⁵ I will visit you after passing through Macedonia, for I intend to pass through Macedonia, ⁶ and perhaps I will stay with you or even spend the winter, so that you may help me on my journey, wherever I go. ⁷ For I do not want to see you now just in passing. I hope to spend some time with you, if the Lord permits. ⁸ But I will stay in Ephesus until Pentecost, ⁹ for a wide door for effective work has opened to me, and there are many adversaries.

¹⁰ When Timothy comes, see that you put him at ease among you, for he is doing the work of the Lord, as I am. ¹¹ So let no one despise him. Help him on his way in peace, that he may return to me, for I am expecting him with the brothers.

Final Instructions

¹² Now concerning our brother Apollos, I strongly urged him to visit you with the other brothers, but it was not at all his will to come now. He will come when he has opportunity.

¹³ Be watchful, stand firm in the faith, act like men, be strong. ¹⁴ Let all that you do be done in love.

¹⁵ Now I urge you, brothers—you know that the household of Stephanas were the first converts in Achaia, and that they have devoted themselves to the service of the saints— ¹⁶ be subject to such as these, and to every fellow worker and laborer. ¹⁷ I rejoice at the coming of Stephanas and Fortunatus and Achaicus, because they have made up for your absence, ¹⁸ for they refreshed my spirit as well as yours. Give recognition to such people.

Greetings

¹⁹ The churches of Asia send you greetings. Aquila and Prisca, together with the church in their house, send you hearty

greetings in the Lord. ²⁰ All the brothers send you greetings. Greet one another with a holy kiss.

²¹ I, Paul, write this greeting with my own hand. ²² If anyone has no love for the Lord, let him be accursed. Our Lord, come! ²³ The grace of the Lord Jesus be with you. ²⁴ My love be with you all in Christ Jesus. Amen.